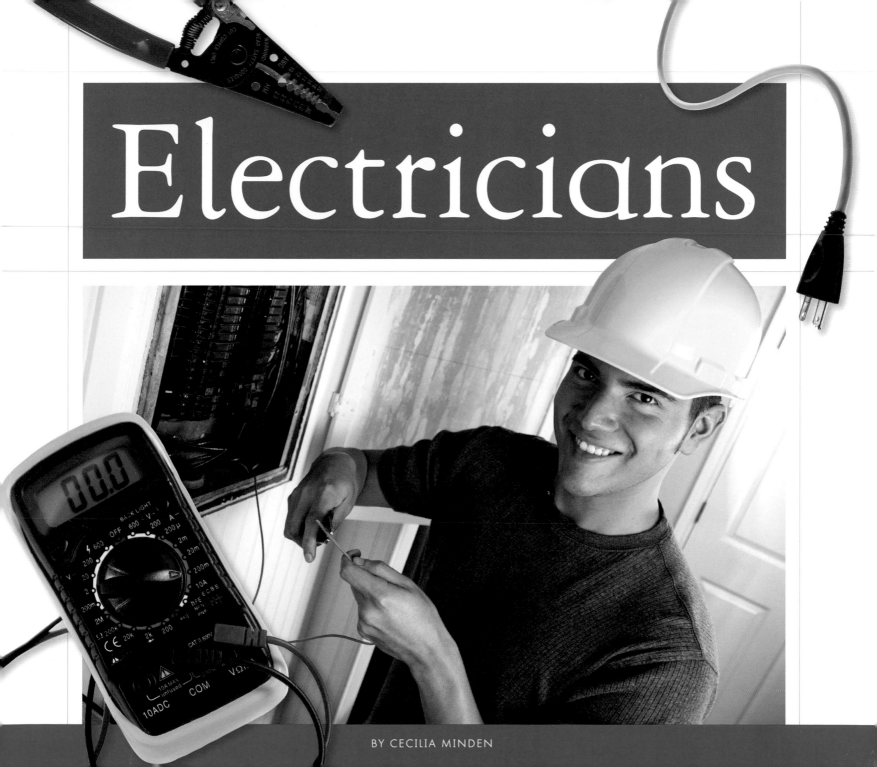

Electricians

BY CECILIA MINDEN

The Child's World

Published by The Child's World®
1980 Lookout Drive • Mankato, MN 56003-1705
800-599-READ • www.childsworld.com

Acknowledgments
The Child's World®: Mary Berendes, Publishing Director
The Design Lab: Design
Jody Jensen Shaffer: Editing
Pamela J. Mitsakos: Photo Research

Photos
auremar/Shutterstock.com: 5; BartCo/iStock.com:
10-11, 20-21; dial-a-view/iStock.com: wire cutters;
fstop123/iStock.com: cover, 1; hartcreations/iStock.
com: 4; lisafx/iStock.com: 12; michaeljung/iStock.
com: 6-7; Monkey Business Images/Dreamstime.com:
8; MrPants/iStock.com: power cord; Photodisc: design
elements; polarica/iStock.com: digital meter; sturti/
iStock.com: 16; tinabelle/iStock.com: 17; T.J.Minden:
9, 14; Viktor Levi/Dreamstime.com: 22; wzhou/iStock.
com: 18

ISBN 9781626870123
LCCN 2013947292

Printed in the United States of America
Mankato, MN
December, 2013
PA02191

ABOUT THE AUTHOR

Dr. Cecilia Minden is a university professor and reading specialist with classroom and administrative experience in grades K–12. She earned her PhD in reading education from the University of Virginia.

CONTENTS

Hello, My Name Is Selena.

Hello. My name is Selena. Many people live and work in my neighborhood. Each of them helps the neighborhood in different ways.

I thought of all the things I like to do. I like to take things apart to see how they work. I like to think of different ways of solving a problem. How could I help my neighborhood when I grow up?

I Could Be an Electrician!

Electricians are good at working with their hands. They know how lots of different parts work together. Best of all, electricians get to work in many different places and figure out interesting ways to solve problems.

When Did This Job Start?
Houses and businesses began using electrical power in the late 1800s. Workers were needed to install electrical equipment.

Electricians know how wiring and many other parts all work together.

Learn About This Neighborhood Helper!

The best way to learn is to ask questions. Words such as *who*, *what*, *where*, *when*, and *why* will help me learn about being an electrician.

Where Can I Learn More?
National Electrical Contractors Association
3 Metro Center, Suite 1100
Bethesda, MD 20814

National Joint Apprenticeship
and Training Committee
301 Prince George's Boulevard, Suite D
Upper Marlboro, MD 20774

Asking an electrician questions will help you learn more about the job.

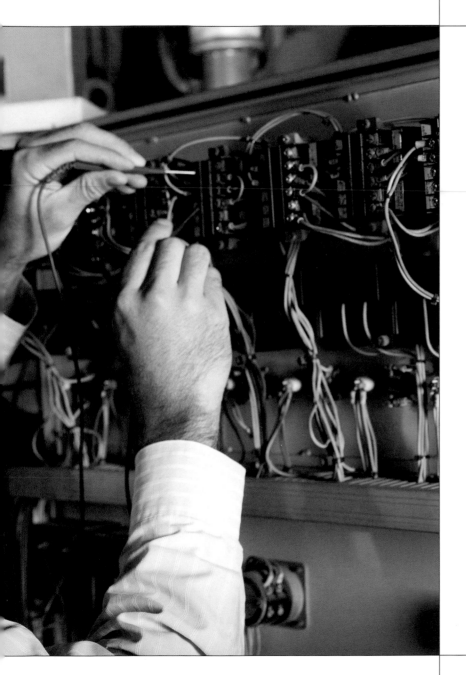

Who Can Become an Electrician?

Boys and girls who like science may want to become electricians. It is also important for electricians to be good at problem solving.

Electricians are an important part of the neighborhood. They keep people's lights and machinery working. Electricity powers everything from refrigerators to computers. Our world would be completely different without electricity!

How Can I Explore This Job?

Working with model trains will help you learn to use many of the tools electricians use. You can also talk to the custodian at your school. Discuss what kind of electrical work he or she does.

Electricians must be good at problem solving.

Meet an Electrician!

This is Manuel Olvera. Manuel is an electrician in Saint Louis, Missouri. He likes being an electrician, but he knows he has to be careful all the time. Electricity is important but can be very dangerous. When Manuel is not working as an electrician, he likes to spend time with his family.

How Many Electricians Are There?
About 659,000 people work as electricians in the United States.

Manuel knows he must be very careful when working with electricity.

Where Can I Learn to Be an Electrician?

Most people studying to be electricians learn what to do by working as **apprentices**. Students in an apprenticeship program often go to classes as part of their training.

Electricians also need a license from the state where they live. But most electricians keep taking classes even after they get a license. Each state has rules

People training to be electricians learn how to read blueprints.

electricians must follow when they are installing equipment in homes or office buildings. Classes help electricians learn the most up-to-date rules.

Someone studying to be an electrician must also learn how to read a **blueprint**. Manuel uses blueprints to help him install electrical equipment.

How Much School Will I Need?

People studying to be electricians must be at least eighteen years old and have a high school diploma. Electricians learn their job by working in an apprenticeship program. These programs last for three to five years. Electricians must also usually pass a test to get a license from the state where they live.

The electrician in the yellow hat is learning about circuit breakers.

What Does an Electrician Need to Do the Job?

Manuel uses many tools on his job. A few of these are screwdrivers, knives, pliers, and wire cutters. Electricians' tools have special insulation on them. This means they have a coating that prevents Manuel from getting hurt by the electricity.

Think of all the things in a home that use electricity. It takes a lot of electrical power to make all of those things work. Homes with electricity depend on **circuit breakers**.

Wire cutters are an important tool for electricians.

What Clothes Will I Wear?

- Work boots
- Work clothes or uniform
- Work gloves

Manuel knows how to install circuit breakers so electricity keeps flowing through people's homes.

Manuel sometimes puts wiring in new homes that are being built.

Where Does an Electrician Work?

Electricians work in many different places. Manuel works with electricity where people are building new businesses. These are called commercial buildings. He also works in new homes that are being built.

Other electricians work in maintenance. Has a big storm ever stopped the electricity in your neighborhood? A maintenance electrician probably fixed the power lines to bring back the electricity.

What's It Like Where I'll Work?
Electricians work both indoors and outdoors. Sometimes they work with circuit breakers inside a home. Other times they work outside and repair damaged power lines.

15

How Much Money Will I Make?

Most electricians make between $31,000 and $55,000 a year.

Manuel's job is different every day. He may be climbing ladders or working outside in bad weather. Sometimes Manuel has to work where it is dirty and hot. Other times he may have to work in a very small space. Manuel must always follow safety rules around electricity no matter what kind of job he is working on.

Electricians often take care of wiring in commercial buildings.

Who Works with Electricians?

Manuel works with carpenters, plumbers, and other electricians when he has a job at a new house. Apprentices also help Manuel and learn from him.

What other Jobs Might I Like?
- Aircraft mechanic
- Drafter
- Engineering technician

Electricians sometimes work with other craftspeople such as carpenters.

The world's largest lightbulb is in Menlo Park, New Jersey.

When Would an Electrician Need Superpowers?

The largest lightbulb in the world is in Menlo Park, New Jersey. It was built to honor the inventor of the lightbulb, Thomas Edison. This "super bulb" is 13 feet (4 meters) tall and weighs 8 tons. An electrician would have to make sure a lot of power was available to light up that bulb!

I Want to Be an Electrician!

I think being an electrician would be a great way to be a neighborhood helper. Someday I may be the one to install electricity in your home!

Is This Job Growing?
The need for electricians will grow faster than other jobs.

These kids are studying electricity in school.

Why Don't You Try Being an Electrician?

Do you think you would like to be an electrician? You can start by learning about different types of electricity. One type is **static electricity**. Have you ever walked across a carpet, touched a metal object, and then felt a shock? This is caused by static electricity.

Blow up a balloon. Try to get the balloon to stick to a wall. It will fall off.

Now rub the balloon on the top of your head and try again. The balloon will probably stick to the wall this time. Static electricity causes this to happen.

Static electricity can make your hair stick out in all directions!

GLOSSARY

apprentices (uh-PREN-tiss-iz) students who learn a trade by working with people who are already skilled in that trade.

blueprint (BLOO-print) a drawing of a house or building

circuit breakers (SIR-cut BRAY-kurz) switches that control the electrical power flowing in and out of a home

static electricity (STA-tik i-lek-TRIS-uh-tee) electricity created by rubbing two objects against each other

LEARN MORE ABOUT ELECTRICIANS

BOOKS

Cast, C. Vance. *Where Does Electricity Come From?* Hauppauge, NY: Barron's, 1992.

Lytle, Elizabeth Stewart. *Careers As an Electrician.* New York: Rosen Publishing Group, 1993.

Overcamp, David. *Electrician.* Danbury, Conn.: Children's Press, 2003.

WEB SITES

Visit our home page for lots of links about electricians:

www.childsworld.com/links

Note to Parents, Teachers, and Librarians: We routinely check our Web links to make sure they're safe, active sites—so encourage your readers to check them out!

INDEX